Car Dealerships Marketing

Richard Halbe

Dedication

I dedicate this book to my wife, Celina, our daughter, Sophia, and my late grandfather, Henrique Halbe.

Acknowledgments

I would like to thank my wife, Celina, for supporting me and encouraging me to write this book. Also, I would like to thank my former employers and bosses who have challenged me by giving me the opportunity to exceed results and excel myself. Special thank you to my former General Manager, Mark Faul, who believed and invested in me.

About the Author

Richard Halbe is a Marketing Strategist, MBA, has a Bachelor's degree in Publicity and Advertising, over twenty years of experience in Marketing, and seven years in Project Management. He has worked for car dealership groups in Canada as a Marketing Manager – increasing traffic, leveraging leads, and growing sales

Contents

Page Let Blank Intentionally

Foreword

"Hi, honey. Do you remember whether I scheduled our vehicle to pick me up tomorrow at 6 pm from work?"

You might find this statement bizarre today, but it will be quite common in the near future. The book will help you with navigating from the present day today, all the way to the distant future. I will share all the knowledge I have accumulated over the years with you, as well as the numerous strategies and results I have learned. I will give you valuable insights into what is coming in the near future and how that will impact your car dealership and its operations.

The market is changing at a breakneck speed. Indeed, you must have heard this several times. You might have said it yourself several times. As a car dealer, you might have felt it yourself. The way customers are buying vehicles today is significantly different than how it used to be and will continue to change for the foreseeable future. Retaining the same traffic level in dealerships has been a massive challenge. Although getting leads has been a temporary solution. To retain existing customers, as well as attracting and satisfying new ones, you need a strong Marketing Strategy. The following chapters will show you how to achieve just that. In a more competitive market with decreasing margins, you need marketing knowledge and plans. There is no easy or quick magical solution. Your dealership needs achievable goals, strategies, marketing plans with frequency and sequence and to track and measure results to adjust plans. Customers are less loyal to a specific vehicle make's brand as compared to others' –at least, that is what research by Michelle Morris, an Automotive Industry Director at Google.

Moreover, a recent study with customers shows that 63 percent of new vehicle purchasers begin their search with a specific brand in mind. However, only 20 percent of shoppers buy the vehicle they first looked up online, while 73 percent of in-market search activities involve cross-shopping. Then, 87 percent of new owners say they are likely to buy the same brand next time around, but only 56 percent end up as repeat purchasers. Based on this study, your dealership should consider investing more time and strategies to retain your customers through an above-average service and customer service.

A designated BDC person would help make that happen, not to mention increasing service appointments and making sales follow up phone calls if your sales associates are not making them. To the customer, this would sound more professional and personalized. If you are wondering where you might find that kind of professional, consider scouting in the hospitality industry.

Before you start implementing these strategies, it is vital that you have someone who has a lot of data-related knowledge. Alternatively, you can call your Customer Relationship Management (CRM) provider to come and visit your dealership to clean, update, and organize your database. Some areas to work on and update include:

- Making sure all orphaned customers are assigned to a specific sales associate. An orphaned customer is one who has gotten part-way through the sales process but was abandoned. You must also delete the names of sales associates who are not working at your dealership anymore.

- Avoid generating reports with incomplete contact information such as phone numbers, email addresses, cell phone numbers, and actual vehicle(s). Use the automated email blast to ask customers to provide updated contact information or ask your sales staff or BDC to contact them for the relevant data. You can also use this opportunity to offer something new or to mention current offers.

- Investigate the actual vehicles. Generate the last closed Repair Orders (ROs) in the last 18 months and cross-reference with the sales report (name, year, make, model) in order to update vehicles per customers so you could avoid contacting customers that your CRM tells you are still driving certain makes and models when they are not.

- Train your frontline staff, Service Advisors, Sales Associates, and Receptionists to ask to confirm customers' contact information every time customers call or visit your dealership.

- Remove the deceased from your CRM to avoid wasting resources and time. Your Sales Associates can help you by providing you this information.

At this point, it is important that you make sure you control and remove customers that asked you to stop calling or contacting them. Neglecting this will only cause trouble and trials for your dealership, which has the potential of spiraling into a Public Relations (PR) nightmare.Once you have your database clean, organized, and healthy, set up follow up tasks and be ready to use messages and scripts that must be used by the Sales Associates and BDC. A way of retaining your customers is having your staff trained to be able to treat each customer individually, using the CRM or database to get information through comments.

Keep in mind that the cost to acquire a new customer is five times higher than retaining a current customer. There are a few things your dealership can do to retain customers:

• Keep your customers informed. Have a monthly electronic newsletter with the latest news, such as new models, the first new model units, community events you hosted or attended, service and parts specials for the month, and loyalty coupons only for actual customers, all with pictures and details attached. If you have a loyalty program or your dealerships run the manufacturing program, promote that about it. Add two or three recent customers' reviews and the latest vehicle deliveries with pictures attached. Of course, make sure you have the customer's consent – a one-page waiver where they could choose to sign when the vehicle is delivered and before the picture is taken. It could go along the lines of, *"By signing this waiver, the customer agrees to have his/her name, review, and image used internally and externally."* Do not force the customer to sign this waiver and leave it up to them to decide. Personalize the newsletter by inserting the customer's first name on it. This is one example of why it is so important to have your database organized and updated.

• Contact your customers on their vehicle's one-month anniversary. You can email, call, or send a card, and could offer something special. For instance, a free car wash. It is an excellent method of fostering goodwill.

• Create a Group on Facebook to have discussions and post news and relevant information about your dealership, and the make and models presently available. You can even create car clinics by having a technician or sales associate answering questions. Indeed, the possibilities are limitless.

Nonetheless, despite making all this effort to serve all your customers through the best strategies, you will still encounter some problems with certain customers, and they will spread the word by writing negative reviews on Google, Dealer Rate, Facebook, Yelp, and other websites. Every time that happens, you must have a strong process in place to first call an emergency internal meeting with managers and staff involved in the incident. This is to know in detail what the issue was and then find an appropriate solution accordingly.

Secondly, a manager should call the customer in order to listen to him or her and present a solution accordingly. You can also choose to reply to the review, letting the public know that the customer was contacted, and all efforts have been made to resolve the problem properly. In any case, you must meet with the involved managers and staff to discuss what could have been done differently to avoid the situation, and use the outcomes to review your process if needed.

These are the fundamentals of what you need to know about running a car dealership today. Of course, it gets far more complicated, and we will discuss that in the chapters to come. Using the tools taught in this book, you will be ready to face the challenges ahead as the market fluctuates and changes to keep pace with consumer demands.

Chapter 1
Strategy and Planning

It all starts with a business plan, the first step for any significant overhaul.

For a start, your dealership will have to gather and analyze some statistics. Information is the key to getting started; otherwise, you will be in the dark. Collect the previous three to five years' worth of data on traffic, inventory, revenue, average gross sales, sales per make and model, sales of used and new models, monthly sales, service, sales of parts, number of ROs (repair orders), parts inventory, achievements, and any other relevant stat. This will help you set goals based on manufacturing data and other internal indicators, such as:

- Market Analysis
- Market Shares
- New Entrants
- New Models
- Customer Retention
- Customer Satisfaction Index

- Market Research
- Previous Business Plans
- Business Investments
- Main Objectives (for e.g., to build a body shop or to expand shop)
- Human Resources Needed to Deliver Next Year's Goal
- Sales per Month
- Budget Reviews
- New Year Budgets (fixed and variable expenses)
- Customer Acquisition Cost
- Cost per Lead
- Number of Leads
- Conversion Rate

Once you have the business plan goals, then you can begin doing the budget for the whole dealership, dividing it according to each department's expenditures.

A marketing budget should be a percentage of your revenue – anywhere from 5% to 10%, according to NADA (National Automobile Dealers Association). As such, a marketing budget is usually anywhere from $600 to $1000 per unit. Using the Marketing Budget Template, which you can find at *www.halbe.ca*, start inputting the sales goals in the units on the bottom of the spreadsheet (new and used). It will automatically calculate the percentage per month.

After this, input the total marketing budget in dollars on the total year field, and the spreadsheet will calculate the monthly budget by itself. You may want to add the number of leads' goals on the top of the Marketing Budget Template (input, then per month based on previous years and expected growth) or use a formula (for e.g., some car dealerships calculate 25% sales from leads and for every four leads, they got one sale). This system improves your efficiency and reduces the chances of human error.

However, before you fill out the Marketing Budget Template, you should analyze what worked and what did not in terms of marketing. Explore all platforms, such as Google Ads, Bing Ads, Instagram Ads, Facebook Ads, Radio, Newspaper, TV, Private Sales, Direct Mail, Events, Sponsorships, Partnerships, and all the other options. To that end, use previous years' data to analyze it (for e.g., the cost per vehicle, number of leads per channel, and syndicated data such as CarGurus, Auto Trader, Kijiji, and others). If you do not have the previous years' budgets, ask your accounting department to provide you with all the relevant information on advertising expenses from previous years, breaking down per month. By doing this, you have just triggered the Marketing Strategy and Plan. Depending on the size and structure of your dealership, you can do it by yourself and then present it to your boss (Dealer Principal and or General Manager) for approval. Alternatively, if your dealership already has a Marketing Team or Leadership team, it is time to set up appointments with them to start working on it.

My recommendation in the scenario when there is a Marketing or Leadership Team is to be prepared. You should first have a Marketing Strategy and Plan version ready to be discussed and reviewed, as that saves time and keeps the dealership on track, avoiding suggestions that did not work in the past as per the data and results analysis you did prior to the Marketing Leadership meeting.

Use the Marketing Budget Template to present your Marketing Strategy, followed by a presentation showing the market and economy overview, competitors' analysis, your business plan's goals in units, revenue from new and used sales, traffic, leads, service sales, parts sales, and body shop sales. If you have more than one dealership branch, then you can further divide this data according to each location. Depending on the situation, you can also collectively present all the data to show how the entire chain of dealerships is performing.

After this, show the previous years' results in terms of leads, units sold, revenue, traffic, private sales, sponsorship, events, partnerships, and direct mails to defend your point and show where to invest and adjust. On the next slide, show your marketing strategy proposal on what to invest and what percentage it would form on the total budget.

Your Marketing Strategy and Plan should consider special dates or events that could drive traffic to your dealership. For instance, imagine your dealership's 25th anniversary is approaching. Consider a 25th Dealership Anniversary Offer. Present the investment needed for this special "offer," whatever it is (Sale? Event? Markdown?), and then think about what advertising strategy you should adopt (Radio? Facebook? Direct Mail? Email?). On the next slide, expound on new models to be launched and what kind of strategy you recommend for them. Also, discuss when to start advertising them, how much money is needed, and who would be targeted. We should also consider the manufacturers' campaigns that you already know will probably be repeated every year (for e.g., employee prices, Black Friday sale, Clearance sale, X% off, First Payment in 90 months, etc.). Include these on your presentation and what you are going to do with them in terms of strategy. Of course, discuss any necessary investments as well. You have noticed that the Marketing Plan is going to be dynamic and will have reviews and adjustments all over the year.

Knowing your audience and customers is the key to improved results. To understand them better, dig into your database or CRM and run reports to find the most makes and models sold to specific demographics divided based on gender, age, area, socioeconomic condition, and more. If you do not have this data, try your best with what you have – such as, use the date of birth to determine the age and proceed accordingly. In any case, this is more proof that it is extremely important to keep your database healthy and updated. Look at the kind of purchase, such as financing, lease, cash, average term, interest rate, city, etc., to gain perspective. You can also take a look at Facebook Insights to find your surrounding area's average age, gender, etc. You can use Google Analytics to determine website traffic, Google ads performance, traffic acquisition, conversions goals, etc.

Then, present what your strategies are in terms of Digital and Traditional Marketing, as well as the investment percentage for each one. If you are going to try something you have never done before, such as advertising on LinkedIn, present and explain what is LinkedIn, who your target audience is, what kind of response you expect, what kind of ads can you do there, what investment figures you are suggesting to allocate, and what results what are expecting.

Break down your Marketing Plan for Digital and Traditional Marketing. Present sponsorships, partnerships, and events you are going to renew or invest in, as well as why the dealership should invest in them (for e.g., the benefits of targeting that specific audience, community engagement, branding, etc.). Bring in ideas that you consider can generate traffic or bring leads and increase sales. You can even consider competitions, such as one where the winner could get a prize or free snow removal during the Winter (I have personally done this before, and it worked). Alternatively, you can also consider a live online appraisal using auction platforms such as TradeRev. Moreover, the important fact is that it has been proven meetings are at peak production level when there are fewer people involved— specifically, no more than eight, according to Harvard.

Finding some areas to change or renegotiate will give you the task of collecting some syndicated data to negotiate if the results were below expected. This is the moment to contact them and negotiate a new contract, reducing or increasing the investment. To this end, the previous year and last three years' data will help with making that decision.

Keep in mind that you may have to review your internal process if it is the case as sometimes, the problem is not with them, but the level of descriptions, pictures, videos, price strategies, and inventories you have as that can affect the performance and how you list on those syndicated data. Once you obtained the new monthly investment from these vendors, input them on the spreadsheet month by month (some of them will charge you per week, so you should consider that some months have five weeks instead of four and will cost you more sometimes). This is the time for adjustments and defining where to invest in and how to utilize your marketing budget. Once approved and finished, schedule the first quarter Marketing Plan meeting review and repeat the process.

Now, it is time to fill out your Marketing Budget Template with the Marketing Plan once the required investment is approved. Just input the figures and make sure you do not exceed the monthly budget you input previously. Keep in mind; your marketing budget can be increased or reduced along the months, so try taking that into account by creating a cushion.

Tracking results is the key to know how and where to cut or increase budgets. Here is a clue: leave a part of the monthly budget for last-minute actions and events. Although I strongly recommend you stick with the plan, things often change, and so does the market. Opportunities arise spontaneously. You might need to sponsor an important event at the eleventh hour. Be prepared for that.

Every month, track your expenses and ask your accountant to provide an expense report. Usually, I allocate most of the budget to digital marketing, such as syndicated data, Google, Bing, Facebook, and Instagram – about 65% or over. Why? Data shows that customers will visit 1.5 dealerships before they buy. According to Google, they researched for an average of thirteen hours online, too. Of course, digital marketing will get you leads, appointments, traffic, and sales. If your car dealership still relies only on traditional marketing, such as newspapers, radio, TV, or flyers, then you must have seen your traffic and sales decreasing throughout recent years. It is time to change (ask me how at *www.halbe.ca*).

No, it is not the economy; it is the new reality of how customers buy vehicles. Keep in mind that there are high seasonal months, such as Spring and Summer, and low seasons, like Winter.

Creating an In-house Campaign

Let us do an In-house Campaign and consider how we could plan it. Perhaps, let us plan a Tax-match Campaign. First, you have to define the campaign, budget it, calendar it, and present it to decision-makers for approval—including those in your Marketing Strategy and Plan meeting presentation. Then, you plan, communicate, train the sales and frontline staff (receptionist, etc.), track, and generate the Return on Investment report (ROI).

Let us do this step by step:

1) If your dealership has teams and groups, bring in this and other ideas to the meeting but have some information collected and research done. Be prepared for questions, and try to sell your idea.

2) If your dealership does not have teams or groups, prepare a presentation for your boss (Dealer Principal or General Manager). Let us start preparing the presentation from this point: Match-Match tax sales event. The first question is how much to match per vehicle sold? New? Used? New and Used? Up to $1,000? Then, think about the date: the end of March and April? Should it end on April 30th? Do you plan to extend it till mid-May? Will it be on all makes all models? Or perhaps, only on selected models or $500 for cars and $1,000 trucks and SUVs? Does your dealership have a $1,000 margin?

Let us say yes, you do. How many vehicles do you forecast to sell with this campaign? Think of the best-case scenario and how it would add to your monthly goal, even if, on average, it helps hit the monthly goal. Why is it important to forecast how many units to sell: to calculate campaign Return on Investment (ROI) and find room for improvement for the next campaign.

3) Define your advertising strategy. In this particular campaign, I would suggest using radio, signage, remote radio with an event on a specific day, Google Ads, Social Media (Facebook Events, Ads, Live Videos on Instagram, etc.), emails to equity position customers, and SMS. Plus, call people with a special invitation for the event with extra markdowns for regular customers (if you have the margin).

4) Once presented and approved, you can budget it on the Marketing Budget Template.

5) One to two months before you can start planning with radio ads, schedule broadcast dates on a spreadsheet (more will be discussed in chapter two). Meet the radio representative in advance, and choose the station that has the general audience you are looking for – we will explore more in chapter two. If you have a graphic designer, it is time to ask him/her to create the artwork for your campaign if you do not have it already. Create it, and do not forget to ask your website provider or webmaster to create and upload the banner, landing page, and lead form to capture leads from your website, which must be live when the campaign starts and removed when it ends. If you decided to extend the campaign, have the artwork ready to be used on the website and your ads.

6) It is four weeks before the campaign starts, and you should communicate and confirm with your boss to get the go-ahead with the campaign unless you already did that during the Marketing Strategy and Plan sessions. Meet the sales managers to align and plan.

7) Work on the radio script – receive, review, and approve. Based on what you think, ask for changes, and then review them once you get them. Submit it for your boss approve once you think it is done. If they themselves have any alterations, get them done as well.

8) Using the artwork, print some posters or decals to put on service two to four weeks prior to the event or first day of the campaign if you have another in house campaign running at your dealership.

9) Create a Facebook event with the campaign (see chapter three).

10) Create your Google Ads prior to the event.

11) If you have a CRM, insert your campaign on it to track customers that came as per the campaign. If you do not have a CRM, ask them to write down the campaign name on the traffic logging book.

12) Once ready, share the event's information (date, offer, etc.) with sales, service, and parts managers and ask them to communicate it with their teams, plus the dealership's reception. Why? Customers see the dealership as one, and having all your staff aware and informed to answer questions from customers about the event (or campaign) helps increase traffic.

13) Prepare a list of FAQ (Frequently Asked Questions) about the campaign, then print or email them to the staff. It should answer most of the important questions, including how to log on to the CRM.

14) One day before the event, make sure all staff is trained. If you have a daily sales meeting, use it to kick off the campaign and answer any questions they may have.

Check if posters are on service. Make sure radio ads will start to advertise. Check your Facebook Ads, Google Ads, and Facebook event page's number of interested participants and confirmed participants. Send out the email blast and or SMS to your customers, enticing them about what is on offer (for e.g., "bought two years before" or older, specific models. Are there only new models, or used, or both? Are there any unique models? It all depends on who your campaign is targeting and what is your offer). Print the equity customers list and prepare scripts and distribute them to sales associates or BDC (Business Development Center) so they can start calling or text messaging.

15) On the first day of the event, stay around on the showroom, monitoring and assisting the sales team. You may want to talk with some customers to ask what brought them in.

16) Every morning, run sales reports and track on CRM and confirm with sales managers to track sales from the campaign.

17) Keep your boss informed on how the campaign is doing and how many sales you have achieved. Work closely with your sales manager's peers for this.

18) If needed, make corrections and adjusts. Meet your boss and sales managers if needed.

Improving your sales will be your first step towards taking your dealership to new heights by bringing it into the 21st century. Changing how you strategize and market, using the aid of digital technologies, will prove immensely helpful. As we move forward with this book, you will gradually become acquainted with even more techniques for maximizing your sales.

Chapter 2
Traditional Marketing Is Dying

Newspaper, Magazine, Radio, TV, Direct Mail, Flyers, Outdoor

You may be tempted to advertise in whatever you *personally* think is the best advertising medium based on your life's experiences. Often, these experiences are steeped in the past, endorsing marketing techniques that are rapidly being phased out. The advertising sector is significantly different today from what it was in the past. Hence, if you have presently allocated dollars to advertise on some traditional marketing medium, such as a Newspaper, hold it, delay the advertisement campaign, and review your decision after you read this chapter.

Newspapers certainly had their importance for decades, but they have lost a lot of that exposure. With the proliferation of the internet and with more businesses using it than ever before, traditional media are struggling to keep up. Businesses around the world are using the internet to promote their products and services. New ways to search, compare, inquire, browse, and buy have emerged, shattering the status quo and changing the way customers shop, giving them the power to compare, search, learn, and buy.

It is widely known now that newspapers have been in decline, especially since the 2000s. Various reasons have been speculated, but most agree that social media and the internet have crucial roles to play in this. I want to make it clear that journalism will survive as it is, but the old printed newspaper simply will not. This is a simple reality that must be recognized at the earliest. My point is to advise you not to spend your budget on newspaper ads if they are printed.

Conversely, bear in mind that I enthusiastically support digital advertising on newspapers' websites (banners ads) to generate traffic to your website and get leads.

This is a good strategy for small communities where people rely on the local community browsing local newspapers' websites, though it can also work for large corporations. All the benefits you can attain by advertising online are automatically gained when you advertise in a newspaper online.

That said, the question of whether newspapers will reclaim their spot as the best advertising platform remains unanswered. Presently, it seems unlikely, as most of them still rely on printed newspapers' ads for a substantial chunk of their revenue. Moreover, with the exceptions of large publishing groups, most of these newspapers do not have the digital culture and knowledge to establish a solid online presence. Usually, their sales team is still trained to try to sell the traditional printed ad, and most of them cannot explain how digital advertising works and how much it costs. Not to mention that it is quite expensive to advertise on it – having good frequency and sequence. Plus, you cannot receive reliable feedback instantly, either.

Another fact to observe and consider is that younger generations, especially millennials, do not read printed newspapers – at least, the vast majority of them. In this cyberspace, advertising in the newspapers will solely target older people. Your marketing budget has to be spent wisely and to generate as many results it could. As such, you have to decide whether catering more or less exclusively to an aging population will be to your advantage or not. Speaking of magazines, there are two scenarios that you ought to think about. One is that there are many magazines also in decline. Some will disappear, whereas others are going digital and exploring social media, having readers follow their updates and engage on their websites. Usually, their channels are Instagram, Pinterest, and Facebook.

The second scenario is that there are local community magazines that bring relevant information to local communities and small towns. They are good to brand your dealership if you have the budget because of their highly specialized penetration. Frequency and sequence is the name of the game. Do not expect to advertise only one time and get many results. It is ideal for you to build your brand in the local community. To that end, using digital billboards and outdoor billboards, when it comes to branding, can be very useful.

The way people watch TV is changing, too. People can access countless channels' websites online and play their favorite shows and news reports. They can use their wireless internet to watch on streaming stickers and boxes, such as Amazon Fire TV, Apple TV, Roku, various cable providers, YouTube, and Facebook. They can watch these on their TV, or even on their smartphone, tablet, and computer – live and on-demand. Viewers now choose when and what to watch, and in some cases, they can skip and avoid ads altogether. The traditional ad your local TV station offers you during the local news or local program segment is watched, in general, by old people, as this is the audience that is predominantly watching local TV stations. Hence, by advertising here, this is the audience you will target.

Large corporations are still advertising on TV with a consistent strategy, carefully considering their audience nationwide and on all devices. Radio is another medium that has been declining for decades now. It was earlier displaced by satellite radio, iTunes, other technologies. Nonetheless, it is still operated even though it is becoming expensive – in the sense that the returns simply do not keep up with the investment.

Radio provides local news, information, and community events. It is admittedly still good to brand, promote offers, and events, but the future is uncertain as new technologies continue to arrive. Soon, it will probably be replaced. I predict that the next disruption will happen when all vehicles start coming with internet on it. That may dramatically alter radio's market share, as big national groups could start broadcasting all over the country like a national station, delivering custom local ads. Listeners would be able to browse and tune to any radio station in the world. YouTube and Instagram IGT (Instagram TV) will play a big role in this scenario as most of the vehicles will have monitors coming as a standard feature.

While the radio is still working, here is my suggestion on how to advertise on it. If you have a budget, carefully choose the radio station that reaches most of the kind of audience you wish to target. For instance, if you want to target truck buyers, you may prefer to advertise on a country music radio or AM radio station.

You could strategically choose to advertise during a program that most truckers would be interested in, such as during an agriculture news talk show or during a weather broadcast. To find out which one to choose, first, you have to have a business plan, marketing plan, and budget – as explained in *Chapter I: Strategy and Planning*. Once you have done that, then you can browse your local radio stations' websites, or you can contact the sales representatives to visit you and to bring the audience. To introduce effective advertising on the radio, you have to have frequency and sequence, which means a minimum of daily spots and the ability to negotiate with them. Usually, I choose to air five to eight ads per day. When there is not enough of a budget left, I carefully choose the schedule and air one to two ads per day when I think they would be most effective. These could be from noon to 1 pm, or at 12:33 pm right after the weather forecast or news— some of the best times for advertising are in the morning and afternoon rush hour. Sponsorship could also be a good option, for example, in the morning from 7 am to 8 am or during news coverage or sports news.

Live remote radio works if you have lead up ads running prior to your event and if you plan what to pitch and offer during the four hours or less of live remote radio when the radio station comes to your dealership. This is ideal when you have an event or offer going on and want to generate as much traffic as possible. Have your staff trained, decide who will be interviewed by the radio station announcer, and discuss what to say every three cut-ins per hour or less. All this will depend on the radio station. Keep in mind that you can generate traffic not only on the day you have the live remote radio but on the following days or week. However, that will depend on how you plan your event and the cut-ins' messages. For example, *"Today, we are hosting a fundraiser BBQ, and until next Friday, all used vehicles will have up to $5000 off. Come visit us today or call to book an appointment!"*

Use spreadsheet software to plan your radio ads on a calendar, with the number of ads per day in a separate column. The spreadsheet should also mention what radio station the ads will play on and what time the ads will be aired. Depending on your car manufacturer, you can get coop dollars if you use the ads they provide for the monthly campaign, which is something I recommend to be taken advantage of by you.

Another advertising method is direct mail flyers, which are getting ineffective as they are costly and annoy customers. In fact, anywhere from 95% to 99% of them throw them in the garbage. Usually, 1% to 5% will react to your direct mail flyers blast, but of that, very few will end up buying a vehicle. Direct mail letters, on the other hand, reach your customers. One would expect this to be an equitable process, but it is not due to the fact that usually, only elderly people reply. Now, it has been replaced by emails and text messages, and will very soon use AI (Artificial Intelligence) to target the right customers that are more willing to buy a new or newer vehicle based on all database information and store interactions available.

Even direct mail agencies are offering more digital private sales and upgrade sales events rather than letters. There are many agencies doing this by offering email blast, SMS, ringless voice./ message calls, outbound calls, and interactive websites – all of which are effective in their own respective ways. Signage is still important to communicate and advertise campaigns in your dealership. The only difference is that in the near future, these signs will be replaced by digital interactive signage that gives customers more information and connectivity with their devices.

One very good example of this is a company I found in the US that has a digital solution for vehicles' price tags, Altierre, and A.I. Digital. Now that we have recognized that traditional methods do not work anymore, you can start learning new and innovative methods to secure the long-term profitability of your business. The first is to establish yourself in the local community firmly.

Chapter 3
Social Community Engagement

The most fundamental thing you need to understand is that your success rests upon the local community's support. Your aim is to expand your market in a highly competitive field. This is no easy feat. However, with the right strategy, you will be able to increase your net profits. For that, you will have to make the community feel like you are the most trustworthy dealer available.

You have to construct the *right* image for your business. When it comes to building a long term reputation in the local community, brand sponsorship and partnership should be part of your marketing strategy and plan. However, before you start sponsoring every organization that comes knocking on your door, you must plan.

First of all, you ought to include sponsorship and partnership strategies and plans as a part of your marketing tactics. Moreover, they also have to be related to the goals you wish to achieve, or in other words, you have to identify potential sponsorships and partnerships that can deliver results. Instead of immediately focusing on generating traffic, sales, or new customers, you should focus on building your reputation so you can differentiate yourself from your competitors. For long-term success, you absolutely have to expose your brand with cross-advertising and even PR (public relations) to generate "Free Publicity."

To find the best organizations to fit into your plans, you have to research. Unless you are new to the community you are based in, probably a couple of organizations' names have come to your mind, and this is a good start. If you are new, then just do your homework, and you should eventually come up with a list of organizations you trust. You should pay special attention to those who frequently sponsor events in the area.

The next step is to extract more information on those organizations you hope to approach and create a spreadsheet to tabulate and input information, such as events, mission, services, audience, pros, and cons. Then, calculate and input the number of expected attendees and members, the data on publicity and exposure, information on board members, and who they are frequently sponsored by. If they are sponsored by any competitors, it is safer to discard them for the time being.

Once you have all the information collected, inputted, and analyzed, you can add it to your marketing strategy and follow the steps outlined in *Chapter 1: Strategy and Planning*. This kind of methodology works very well if you are committed to having medium and long-term plans. With that said, don't expect to receive instant results.

To maximize results and brand exposure, you have to engage and work actively with the organization to leverage your exposure to the community. Moreover, you should allocate a specific budget to this task, and not only the sponsorship cost (package). You need to have an investment amount ready to include in the planning cost these events and their communication in your advertising.

You should engage all your staff to join you as a part of a dealership project, as well. A united front is important because it is likely that your staff belongs to the community, too. If they feel like they are a part of your brand, you will begin seeing positive benefits rippling across the target market. As such, you must have everyone participating and engaging in utilizing the potential. Once you have target sponsors listed and your staff's support, start drafting your plan using the information and options available to you. A clearly outlined plan is fundamental to get great results. Let us use a real example to illustrate how to do it. There is no limit to excel.

In one of the dealership groups that I worked for, an opportunity knocked on the door one day. The car manufacturer had announced a new organization partnership and sponsorship, specifically a National Paralympics Organization that supports special kids and young people to enroll in one of many sports and provides support to their parents.

When I first came across this bulletin, I instantly retained the information and input it into my documents: Marketing Ideas and tasks list. After I have studied and found that it could be a good strategy to generate more traffic and attract new prospects, I started to research and collect information. I contacted the Organization President and Marketing Director to set up a meeting. Later, I collected additional information during the meeting, as well as some ideas of events and promotions that surged in popularity. The first suggestion was to organize an event with the athletes at the dealership within every few months. I updated my notes accordingly and studied, preparing a presentation, and meeting my general manager at the earliest. I highlighted the pros and cons of the event and managed to get the approval to go ahead successfully. In this case, since it was a national partnership, there was not any contract or negotiation to be done as per the national agreement with the manufacturer.

With this example, you can see how you could typically go about launching an event to attract the local community's interest. At this point, you can see that yes, all marketing strategies and plans have a process to follow once a year and every quarter, but since this is a dynamic industry and some opportunities will appear suddenly, you should make use of them and include them in your marketing plan and budget. It is because of this unpredictability that I encourage you to have a budget buffer to bed that. Later, I met the organization again and presented a detailed plan with three events: one in three months with fundraiser BBQ, a Halloween Fundraiser Event, and Customers' Christmas Event with suggested dates, cost, required human resources, social media strategy, logistics, and organization.

A mere couple of weeks later, we met again to confirm the date for the first event and agree on cross-promotion. We decided that for every new or used vehicle sold during the campaign's promotional period, $250 per each vehicle sold was donated to the organization. Plus, all of the profit from the BBQ event went to them. We bought all meals, condiments, and pops from our budget, but the profits went to them.

It looks simple now, but that project took five months to be crafted, detailed, and approved. Our advertising strategy included radio, live remote radio during the event, Facebook events, Facebook advertising, Facebook and Instagram posts, live Facebook video interviewing the athletes, local organization members, signage, and emailed invitation blasts to all customers. Then, to make sure the event got as much attention as possible, I invited the media to cover the event to generate PR. Consequently, local newspapers and TV came to the event.

The organization and I discussed and agreed to have the athletes bring their banner and promotional material during the event. A table was set up for them, and they cross-posted the event and campaign on their Facebook and Instagram pages, email blasting all athletes, parents, and members.

The event generated huge traffic, and we sold 50% more vehicles than usual on a regular busy Saturday. All the staff was trained and communicated in advance about the event. Besides this, the other two events generated more results. We built a long term relationship with this organization, and even had the manufacture acknowledging it and recognizing the result.

The more you can get involved in the community, the better it is for your brand. It helps create ties with the community and get free publicity. The objective is to boost your exposure and build a reputation. This is a long-term tactic and takes time to start harvesting results. However, you can be confident that the profits will be sustained and rewarding. In my experience, this will especially make a massive positive impact in small and medium cities.

Another example of how to engage and support the community is to open your doors to an organization to use your facility to host an event. Be part of the community by sponsoring local organizations having your brand advertised on their events and sites and posted on their social media and website.

Chapter 4
Social Media Marketing – Have a Strong Social Media Presence

"I bought this from a Facebook page."

Sounds familiar? How many times have we heard someone say this particular line? It's hard to count. Currently, social media has become so popular and common that it rarely fazes us when someone says that they got a certain product via Facebook or any other social networking platform. The marketing on social media has integrated to such an extent that there is no longer a limit to what you can get from there. How should a car dealership be any different? It is not.

The question may arise, how an intermediary, such as a car dealership, sell on Facebook? Or scratch that, how a business that deals in such grand products or services gains benefit out of social media? Is delivery even possible? All of these are valid questions, but with one simple answer. Social Media for a car dealership is to create buzz, generate online traffic, and get the word going around about your dealership. You can also set up "Shop" on social media for people to take advantage of the option, especially for those who already know what they want to buy and don't need a physical visit. However, the use of social media just to market your service is also a great way to attract more customers into your shop.

When it comes to social media marketing, like any other form of marketing tactic, the most important thing first and foremost is devising up a Social Media Marketing strategy. As we have already discussed in previous chapters, the first step to setting up a social media marketing outlay is to have a strategy.

For example: in the case of a car dealership, your social media marketing strategy could be to attract more of your target market so they can avail your goods or services instead of your competitors'. Or to increase word of mouth for your business, so there could be more traction into your shop. Once your strategy is set, the next step is to create an action plan on how to implement the strategy effectively and efficiently. In regards to social media marketing, the most important thing to consider is the outlet you will be using to market your business or set up your shop. As of today, your most adequate and effective options are:

- Facebook
- Instagram
- LinkedIn
- Snapchat
- Twitter

Once you have your platforms shortlisted, you need to evaluate which one would be the main marketing outlet for your dealership. In order to do so, first, you need to know everything about your target market. Such as, what age group should your target market be? What gender? Where should they be from? And their general preferences in cars - luxury, economical, new or used. To summarize, you need to fully be aware of the demographics of your targeted customers. This is important because that way, you can choose one platform to be your main marketing hub, and the rest can either have little to no marketing.

All these social media sites have statistics of people in terms of age groups, location, gender, and more. For example: As per the statistics collected from a dealership

Facebook page, as of April-2020, 20% of Facebook users are men between the ages of 25-35. The rest of the 80% is divided into small numbers among both men and women between the ages of 18-65. For a car dealership, your general target market should be at least above 25 years of age so they can afford to make an investment like buying a car. Given that Facebook is an ideal place to begin your social media marketing plan, this chapter will explain in detail how you can set up your Facebook page for your car dealership in order to maximize your customer traction and generate more sales with the help of few simple social media marketing tactics.

Step by Step Guide to Create your Car Dealership's Facebook Page

The first step in creating a Facebook page for your dealership is to have a personal account. After you have created your personal account, you can then create a business page for your dealership. Once through, you will be prompted to choose a category. The categories are: Business, Venues, Nonprofit, Politicians, Services, Restaurants & Cafes, Shopping, Video Page, Standard. I recommend you to choose the Shopping category option.

The next step is both simple and crucial. This is where you provide all the information about your business. As a car dealership, you are operating in the service sector. After choosing that from a drop-down menu, you will be prompted to state all the necessary details: Company's name, Contact Information, Working hours, Address, etc.

Another important aspect to take care of while putting in your details is the visuals. It's essential to have a relevant, and eye-catching Profile Picture, and cover photo. Most businesses keep updating their cover photo with their promotional campaigns, because it is recommended to keep your profile picture as your logo, so it could be distinguished by your customers. Remember, an image is the first thing a human mind perceives. Make sure you have such that leaves a lasting remembrance of your business in your potential customer's mind.

Next, you need to write your story in the About Us section. This is something that a visitor may read last, but if it's read, a good story instantly captures the customer. This is the section where you tell your customer about your values and how you do business dealings. Your words here will have a great impact on their purchase decision, so spend some good amount of time on this step. Not many businesses know about this, but Facebook allows you to stock your inventory on to your page from the option of Shop. It's important to do that because, in the current times, more and more people are shifting to online shopping. If a page grants them access to all the things they could find physically, online, it instantly increases the chances of a browse being converted into a sale.

When it is all set, you need to make your first post. This one could be an introductory post of who you are and what you offer. Because after the page is published and boosted, this post will be appearing on users' timelines. Make sure that this post directly caters to your target population. This one needs to be straight forward and just enough to get the point across.

Once your page is up and running, it's all about implementing your social media marketing strategy through your previously set action plan.

How can you use Social Media Marketing to your Benefit?

Social Media Marketing, if done right, could prove to be quite beneficial for your business. Whether you're in the service sector, or manufacturing, using social media to market your business is one of the most effective and cost-friendly ways of marketing in the present times. With the widespread surge in the use of social media over the past decade, this is the place that will get the word out about your business to the maximum number of people.

The number one thing to remember when using social media marketing is to have a constant and active presence on your chosen platform. In the case of a car dealership, if you have a Facebook page, you need to make sure that it is very active and regularly updated.

This means that any changes that your company goes through should be updated on the page instantly, such as your contact information, if ever changed, should be your priority to be updated on your page. The page should also cover all your upcoming deals or offers. Delays in doing so will cost you in losing sales and valued customers. One thing is more specific to having a car dealership Facebook page, and that is a pre-set rule book or guidelines. A car dealership acts as an intermediary that provides a service to customers to buy different brands of cars from under one roof. Because of the nature of the car dealership business, it's essential to have guidelines that cater to both the manufacturer and the dealership. Whoever you appoint to manage your social media pages should be made clear of these guidelines prior to advertising your business on social media.

Social Media was primarily created to communicate with one another. This notion is not so much different in business pages, either. The Facebook page of your dealership should also serve as a source of communication with both the current client and a new potential one. This is one of the most effective ways that you can take advantage of social media marketing.

Using Facebook Messenger Right

One thing that makes Facebook the ideal place for social media marketing is the feature of Inbox (Messenger). This place has both in-coming and out-going capability, which means visitors can contact you directly with their queries, and you can respond to them in real-time. Such fast action and reaction make the relationship stronger, and the customer feels they are being heard.

Another great thing about Facebook Messenger is its customization feature. You can personalize the first message that is automatically sent from your end anytime that a client approaches you. One thing that could be done is to pre-set a series of questions, in an FAQs kind of manner, in order to give the customer a quick way to interact with the company. For example: For a car dealership's Facebook page, the first message could be automated to say:

"Hi! Are you looking for a used car or new?"

Since this is the most common category that divides the various cars, this one is a simple way to start off a conversation. The message then could be followed by more questions like:

"Your brand preference?"

"Which year's model would you prefer?"

So on and so forth...

You can also send an automatic message that states:

"Thank you for getting in touch with us! Unfortunately, we are not here at the moment. But we will get back to you soon! Our working hours are (start:00 to end:00)."

This makes the customer know that they are being heard. No response is always worse, so it is recommended that such automatic messages should be pre-set to make the interactive process flow more smoothly.

Making a Social Media Marketing Calendar

Have you ever heard of the words "Marketing Calendar"? There is nothing too scientific or technical about it. This works essentially the same way as a personal planner would. If you are someone who likes to plan ahead for weeks or even months, you would understand the concept of Marketing Calendar. When you have a Facebook page for your car dealership, you should post actively in order to remain visible to your target audience. To do so, you should create a calendar of 365 days, divide it into days-weeks-months. Ideally, you need to post at least three times a week, but it could be more, depending on certain days.

For example, there would be weeks when you will have to post more because you will need to communicate special offers due to upcoming occasions, such as Black Friday or Boxing Day. This is when your posts' number would naturally increase from at least three posts per week, to say three posts in a day.

These changes aside, having a pre-set calendar makes it simple for anyone managing your page to follow through. Plan your when, why, what, and how before you post anything. Figure out the exact date and time for the post, the reason behind publishing the post, what it will include, and how you will arrange it. For instance, should your post intend to offer a Christmas discount (why), you would want to publish it a week before Christmas (when).

Will you include images or videos in the post? (what) Do you have someone who could design the graphics for the images or the videos? (how) You should create your calendar based on answers to these questions. Doing this pre-emptively will lower your risk of mistakes because you will have a clear guideline to follow throughout the year.

Making the Right Post

The most crucial, and most essential part of social media marketing is making that right post which resonates with your target audience. To narrate how intense this could be, I am sharing an example of something that happened to me long ago.

I was a consultant at a car dealership, where I had been appointed as the Social Media (Facebook page) Manager. Remember, we discussed earlier that it's important to market your service after identifying your target population. When I took charge of the company's Facebook page, I began checking the demographics of the majority of the visitors.

The car dealership was located at the countryside. Since it was a rural area, the dealership's intended target market was men between the ages of 30-50, belonging from nearby vicinities. However, when I checked the stats, it turned out that the majority of the visitors of that page were young women, both from the countryside and the city. Because the majority of the visitors were not actual buyers, there was little to no sales generated from the page. The reason for this was that the posts that the page was posting previously were catering to the female gender more than the male. Hence, each post was attracting young women instead of gaining the attention of our targeted demographic, which could have proven fruitful for the business. It was a challenge on my part to turn the whole page around and make it men centric, so more of our target audience could appear on the page. This is the importance of making the right post.

Seasonal Posts: Talking about the right posts, it's also essential for the posts to be well-timed. The whole when and what phenomenon applies to make posts. A seasonal post is a must.

Other than that, posts on trending topics promote products well.

You should always be on a lookout for what's popular among the general public, but specifically your targeted audience. This way, you will be able to tailor-make the posts to fit directly to what they are looking for, or what would be most relatable for them.

Managing Client Reviews

Social Media is a two-way communication device. In the process of creating a page for your car dealership, which caters to your customer's needs and wants in the best way possible, don't forget to focus on the reviews. While making posts is your way to communicate about your service, a review is a customer's means for feedback to your service. Knowing what you're doing right, or where you lack directly from your clients is a really helpful way to improve your business model.

While both positive and negative reviews are important for your business, negative reviews are the ones you need to keep an eye out for more intently than on the positive reviews. This is the feedback that you need to look out for, because this is an opportunity for you to be better, and revaluate your processes.

Companies that take negative reviews in the right way are always one step ahead of those who falsely thrive on just positive feedback. This is why it's called constructive criticism because it constructs you and makes you better than before. One way to handle a negative review when you get one is first to be very prompt in your response. Just as soon as you get it, respond to the public forum. A possible response could be:

"We apologize that you have had a bad experience with us. One of our representatives will be contacting you shortly to resolve the issue. We will ensure you have a satisfying experience in the future."

After that, stay good on your word and really contact the customer. You can do that via Facebook messenger, or if they have provided a number on their account, make a call. Once through, the first thing you need to do is Ask. Disappointed customers usually want someone to listen to their complaints, which is why this is of great importance. You need to listen to what went wrong during their visit. Do the needful to satisfy your clients. Afterward, don't forget to post a follow-up comment on their review stating:

"Thank you for your valuable feedback. We hope your concerns are resolved. We look forward to a long and mutually beneficial relationship in the future with you."

Reviews are something that most new visitors go to check right away. Negative reviews could have a detrimental impact on your business. However, if they are handled positively, they would have an even better effect than positive reviews. This is why never let any bad review go unanswered. Additionally, like it was previously stated, this is also an opportunity to revisit your plans and see what's not working or what needs a little tweaking around. In any business, this is called reviewing your performance. Most big companies do that regardless of negative reviews. However, through social media, this self-review is made easier and more convenient.

Endorsements

Finally, endorsements work like magic for social media marketing. The main purpose of social media marketing is to gain traction, capture a grander audience, and create word of mouth for your service. There are companies that hire people specifically to endorse their brand online through social media.

Have we not seen our fair share of famous people making posts about so and so brands? All those are just endorsements that these people are paid for. However, there is one more effective way of doing this. You need to be on the lookout for someone who has at least a little social media influence. See if this person is naturally interested in your service. Finding someone who already loves what you do, and has been creating word of mouth for you without charging, that is the best win you could ask for. All you need to do here is cash it out more.

"This is not sponsored, I genuinely like this product, and I use it all the time."

Have you ever heard a social media influencer say things like that? Sure enough, yes. It is true. Since we're all consumers, there's a good chance that you will find someone who has an audience of their own and is your loyal customer as well. Who has maybe recently purchased a car from you, and had been impressed by your service. This is the person you're looking for. This is the endorsement in the best way possible.

Contact this person and make a deal with them. Since they are already saying good things about you, paying them to do it would only make them happier and more inclined to endorse your services. This would increase traction on your page further.

Ultimately, social media marketing is one of the most effective marketing tactics of present times. It's the most beneficial branch of Digital Marketing, and it paves the way for a lot of advertisement opportunities in terms of using the digital medium to commercialize your product or service.

Chapter 5
Digital Marketing – Getting Leads

The main purpose of marketing, be it in any form, is to generate leads, which bring in more sales. Previously, we discussed how we can use the online platform, specifically social media, to stay connected with the customers. However, the vast field of digital marketing goes deeper than that. In present times, digital marketing works the same way as conventional marketing did. Perhaps even better, as in the digital age, online platforms have a greater reach than TV.

One of the greatest advantages of digital marketing, in comparison to conventional marketing, is that you can easily carry out all the steps yourself, in a cost-efficient way. TV ads may have been one of the most effective means of advertisement for decades, but they are expensive. This has made it impossible for small businesses to advertise on TV. In contrast to it, digital marketing provides a relatively easy and cost-friendly route to the advertisement. For example, if you are planning to advertise your car dealership on YouTube, you don't have to hire a professional crew to shoot your video. There is no need for a high-end professional camera either. An effective video can be created even at home. Likewise, you don't have to spend big bucks to advertise on a digital platform like one would have to on TV. Digital marketing is budgeted and easy to process.

In this chapter, we will discuss how to use digital marketing for your dealership effectively to get leads and generate sales.

Video Marketing: How to Make a Video

Before diving into the technical details of advertising across various digital platforms, it is important to know how to make the right video ad. This is the most crucial step in your digital marketing because everything else depends on the content you post. The right content in your video, catering directly to your customers' needs and interests will prove very effective for your dealership. Here we will learn all about video making and using your content to your advantage. That is, to promote, show, and highlight your dealership, ultimately leading to sales.

Decide Your Purpose

Every good digital marketing campaign begins with deciding the purpose. Before you continue the process, you need to realize that you are putting in a lot of time, effort, and money into giving your customers an amazing audio-video experience. First, you need to be clear about what you aim to achieve. What do you want your customers to do after they see your video?

Here are a few possible answers to the questions.

- Make a purchase.
- Download something.
- Reach out to you.
- Become aware of your business.
- Perceive your business positively.
- Share your content with others.

The response you seek from your customers can determine the kind of video you choose to create. Having a clear purpose will set the right course of action for you. For example, if your aim is to get customers to contact you, your video could be infomercial about your dealership, which should have your contact information.

Have a Script Ready

Now that you know the purpose of your video, it's time to prepare the script for your video ad. Your script is the personality of your video ad, so it pays to take time and think through your script. Here are a few things that the script of your video should cater to.

- It should tell a story of your car dealership, to create awareness of your business.
- It should connect with your customers.
- It should motivate people to take action that you wish them to take. (Contact the dealership, make a visit, purchase, and recommend to others).
- It should be engaging and gripping.

Create a Storyboard

Your script is essential, but it's just words. You're making a motion picture, so it's a good idea to think through what you want your script to look like on screen. In the film, this kind of script conception is called a *storyboard.* Well-drawn storyboards can be convenient to your cameraman because they specify motion that will happen in that precise shot.

For example, a storyboard for your car dealership may look something like this.

First Frame: A sales manager appears in the frame and greets, "Hello, I am the sales manager at Lakeview Car Dealership." He touches the black SUV. "Come with me on a tour. I'll show you around."

Second Frame: He leaves the indoor area to go out into the showroom.

Third Frame: He walks around as he shows each car that the dealer has.

Fourth Frame: He talks directly to the camera again and narrates all the promotional offers that the dealer is currently having.

Fifth Frame: He gives out the necessary information about the dealer. (Contact number, email, address, etc.) which also displays on the screen in text.

A general storyboard looks something like this, with a frame-to-frame breakdown. It is usually drawn to give a better perspective to the creative team to shoot the ad.

Select Your Filming Time/Location and Equipment

Next, you need to figure out all the practical details. Like at what time should you film? At what location? What equipment should you use? While time and location could be easy picks, the equipment needs to be evaluated properly. Here is a list of some equipment you may use to film.

Camera: A phone's camera or a professional one that is your call to make.

Audio: You need to make sure that your camera can pick the audio clearly. If not, use a secondary device for audio.

Lightening: Make sure that the location you are filming in is well-lit. Otherwise, use stage lights to enhance the frames of your ad.

Extra Props: See if you need anything extra to film.

Film, Edit, and Upload

Finally, when all the intricacies are dealt with, it is time to implement and film. Once you have your video ad ready, it is time to edit the video. This is a sensitive stage. You can add things that can make or break your entire campaign. Some add screen texts, some background music, while others resort to dramatic effects. No matter what you choose, make sure you are steering clear of possible copyright infringement. Don't add any music or effect that you don't have permission for.

Go Live

Other than making a video, one additional possible way of digital marketing is going live on Facebook, YouTube, and Instagram. Although this does not require as many steps as making a video, you should not be too casual about the process, if you wish for it to work in your dealership's favor. First, you need to evaluate the right time to go live. Determine the location of most of the people in your target audience. Then, as per that, go live so the majority of them could attend. It is best if you announce on your page a few days or at least a few hours before going live.

For your dealership, you can do a lot in a live video that could attract your customers. For example, you can give a live tour of your shop. Have your sales manager interact with the audience live and answer all their queries in real time. You can also use live videos to give tours of the cars you have in your inventory. This kind of interactive experience will resonate with the customers and increase your website and store traffic, consequently leading to higher sales.

Once your video is done, a more crucial stage arises, to advertise it on the right platform. Mainly, the digital space has three to four big platforms that you can market your dealership on, once your video is created. They are:

- YouTube
- Facebook
- Instagram (IGTV)

We will be discussing Google, YouTube, and Facebook in detail. This chapter will grant you a thorough guide on how you can advertise on these platforms effectively to get leads and generate sales for your car dealership.

Advertising on Google

Google Ads is an online advertising platform that allows companies to pay the price for their ads to be displayed on Google Search Engine Results Pages (SERPs) and across Google Display Network. Google Ads is one of the most effective digital marketing platforms because it is primarily the one that the customer opens with the intent to *buy*. Google will direct them to ads catering to their search. In recent times, Google is the first stage of the buying process. The customer starts their research here, unlike Facebook or even YouTube, where a customer rarely goes with the intent to buy. In such a case, when an ad is shown to them in the middle of their other activities, some take it as an interruption and are often repelled by it.

For example, if a customer wants to purchase a car, if they know what car they need to buy, they will search for good dealerships close to him. If they have no clue what to buy, they will look for cars with keywords like small cars, sports cars, SUVs, family cars, and more. Google will direct them to websites catering to their search. This is where Google Ads plays a role.

Step-by-Step Guide to Advertise with Google Ads

Set up a Google Ads Account: The first step to advertise on Google Web is to have an account on Google Ads. To do so, you can visit the homepage of Google Ads and follow along the steps there to set up an account.

Set a Goal: The next step is to establish your primary goals. Is your main objective to raise brand awareness? Is it to drive traffic to your website? Do you want to increase conversions? That is, click on your ad to actual sales. It is important to be clear about your goal prior to launching your ad because Google Ads asks you to specify it at the time of setup. It will give you a list that has more options and you will have to select one before you move forward. If you are unsure about your main purpose, it will be difficult to gauge success.

Identify Your Target Audience: You may have more than one goal, and likewise, you may have many audience subsets. When you are beginning the process of advertising, it is important to see everything in broad terms. For example, who do you want to see your dealership ad? How old are those people? Possibly young adults. Where are they located? Mostly in the city, where your physical shop is. Which device do you think they use? Young adults mostly use mobile phones, so the ad needs to be visible and accessible through that.

Create Target Keywords: Picking the right keywords is extremely important to Google Ads' success. Take your time here to research properly. This is crucial. To make things easier, you can use Google Ads Keyword Planner. It is a helpful tool. Also, make sure that you are using a variety of different types of keywords. The various types are Broad Match, Phrase Match, Exact Match, and Broad Match with modifiers.

Set Your Budget and Detect Your Limits: It is important to set up your budget prior to starting. Google will only charge you when someone clicks on your ad.

Create the Ad: Your ad should attract the customers to click on it. When they do, you need to have them land on a user-friendly and attractive page on your website.

Keep Conversion Tracking on: This data is important for determining campaign success and ensuring that you are spending the marketing budget in effective places.

Advertising on YouTube

Stats show that 84% of the consumers end up buying something after watching the ad on YouTube. This proves the effectiveness of YouTube as an ideal digital marketing platform.

Upload Your Video on YouTube

Before you proceed, you need to have these two accounts up and running. In case you already have these in place, you can skip this step and get to the next one.

Create Your New Campaign / Select a Goal

Here you will have to head over to your Google Ads account. You'll find a *Campaign* tab on your left side. When you click on it, you'll get another option of *the New Campaign.* You need to click on it.

Once you have created a new campaign, Google will give you a list of goals and ask you to select from them. Your options will include:

- Leads

- Website traffic

- Sales

- Brand awareness and reach

- Product and brand consideration

- App promotion

For a car dealership, I recommend you to select leads.

Select Your Campaign Type

You will get a few options to choose from: Search, Display, Shopping, Video, Smart, and Discovery.

Choose Keywords

Before you create your ad, you will be asked to select the right keywords.

Create Your Ads

Ads should be attractive and should generate clicks, leads, and conversions. Choose carefully on which page to land after prospect clicks on your ad.

- Have a call to action, like call now, click to browse our inventory

- Have an offer

- Select where to target, choose audiences

- Set up budget

- Setup conversions

Advertising on Facebook

Facebook is another widely visited platform that has been proven to be highly effective for small, medium, or even large businesses. Facebook owns Instagram, WhatsApp, and Messenger. This means when you choose Facebook as your primary medium of advertisement on a digital platform, you will be covering many bases.

Types of Ads on Facebook

Here are some common types of ads that Facebook allows:

- Brand awareness

- Reach

- Traffic

- Engagement

- App Installs

- Video Views

- Lead Generation

- Messages

- Conversions

- Catalog Sales

- Store Traffic

A Guide to Advertising on Facebook

Advertising on Facebook is effective and cost-friendly if you do it right. Meaning, you need to evaluate your goal, target market, and then look for the right Facebook ad that would prove the most advantageous for your business. For a car dealership, we will focus primarily on Lead Generation ads. The steps that you need to follow to advertise on Facebook are:

Create a Facebook Business Page: The first step to advertising on Facebook is to have a business page. You can't advertise without it. Make sure to create one with your dealership name, so that it is distinctive and identifiable.

Decide on Your Objective: Like in YouTube and Google advertisement, Facebook also requires you to have an objective set prior to starting the advertising process. Here is a list of objectives that Facebook allows you to choose from.

- Brand awareness

- Reach

- Lead generation

- Website traffic

- Engagement

- App installs

- Video views

- Conversions

- Messages

- Catalog sales

- Store traffic

To have Facebook ads work effectively in favor of your car dealership, you need to pick one of the following depending on your objective: brand awareness, website and store traffic, lead generation, reach, and conversions.

Once the objective is set, Facebook lets you name the campaign. This is helpful when you have multiple campaigns running on one single page. It becomes easier to identify and separate them when targeting those to your audience.

Targeting the Audience: You can start by putting in the information, like age group, location, gender, and language. As you make your selections, keep an eye on the audience size indicator on the right of the screen, which gives you a sense of your potential ad reach.

Your selections, specific to a car dealership, could ideally be the ages of 25-60, with SUVs and cars, living near your store's location.

Choose Your Ad's Placement: Facebook allows a variety of platforms, out of which you can choose to place your ad. However, if you're unsure of where the ad should be placed, Facebook also has an option of Automatic Placement.

If you wish to pick these details yourself, here are the options that Facebook allows you to choose from:

- Device type: Mobile, desktop, or both

- Platform: Facebook, Instagram, Audience Network, or Messenger

Set Up Your Budget and Schedule Your Ad: Once you are done with every step in the process, you need to set up your budget. You can choose a daily or lifetime budget. Then set the start and end dates if you want to schedule your ad in the future or choose to make it live right away.

Finalize Your Campaign and Publish the Ad: With everything set in order, all there is left to do is post your ad. Facebook is proven to generate leads for car dealerships in the past. The platform is also proven to increase both website traffic and store traffic.

Digital marketing is gaining popularity rapidly. With a grand shift of businesses to online platforms, a service-oriented industry such as a car dealership needs to follow suit. It is the general principle of evolution. Those who don't change with time often go extinct. It is the right time to use digital marketing to get more leads for your car dealership and convert as many of your ad clicks to sales as possible.

Chapter 6
Shifting Your Business Online

"Let me check the options available online first."

This is one sentence that we have become accustomed to both hearing and saying on a regular basis. Even the most service-oriented companies that require physical interaction have started to depend heavily on an extensive online presence. Why? Because it is a demand of the present time. As per current market trends, there aren't many dealerships that are offering FULLY online experience to help customers explore AND BUY cars and avail after-sales services.

Many companies over the past decade have made a complete shift and brought their businesses online. Others have partially made the shift, as they are still operating physically for certain activities. For example, service-oriented industries such as Beauty Salons, or spas have made it easier to book appointments through their pages or websites, but it's necessary for the customer to visit their place of business to avail their services. On the flip side, many retailers, such as Wish, or She-Inn are only operating online, having no requirement of a physical presence at all.

In respect of a car dealership, making a complete shift to online operations could be tricky. However, with correct planning and effective implementation, it is possible. This chapter will discuss how you can make the shift, without compromising your business model or losing existing or prospective clientele.

As per current market trends, there aren't many dealerships that are offering online channels to help customers explore cars of their choice from the comfort of their homes, which is why it is the right time for you to shift your business primarily to an online platform. In doing so, your dealership will be the pioneer of the trend and thus become the innovator. It is that classic case of first-mover advantage over the new entrants, or potential competitors.

Yes, you may ask, "Aren't there already dealerships who are doing that?" Of course, there are some, but the number is so limited that it will still prove advantageous if you choose to take the online route. For example, there's one company in Canada called Clutch, which is selling vehicles online and delivering them at home. Clutch is a great example of understanding the importance and effectiveness of having an online presence for your car dealership.

To understand it better, one can also look at the model that Tesla follows. Many of you may already be aware that Tesla does not have a relevant physical presence. It deals with customers online through its various channels, such as their website, e-mails, social media pages, and more. A customer can go on their website, select their desired car, make personalized changes in it, or order their custom-made car within minutes. Tesla then delivers the vehicle to the customer. It has been proven through the immense success of Tesla that in present times, a strong online presence works wonders, whether you have physical existence or not.

When flowing against the current of the latest market trends, one needs to be careful about the customers they are dealing with. Here, you need to realize that you're mostly dealing with millennials. They prefer to shop online, from small purchases to big purchases like buying a car. The market trend in a car dealership is slowly taking a shift for that very reason. Because this industry has long been based on a physical shop only, the shift could be a hard one. It needs careful planning and strategic thinking. The question to answer here is, 'What could a car dealership do to be ready for this?'

Shifting Your Business Online

If someone told you that you need to redesign your entire business model and re-write all your strategies to survive in an online business environment, you would feel overwhelmed. Making this shift is huge, and it is not something that could be done overnight. No! We do not have a magic wand. Having the right mindset toward your goal is the first step to achieve anything.

This is why the first thing that you need to do is to treat this business shift as a project rather than a 360-degree redesign of your business model. That way, you will automatically feel less stressed, and it will become easier to tackle the shift to an online platform. Like any other project, the online shift of your business will also have steps that you need to follow carefully. The first step is to seek permission from all your stakeholders - Managers,

Owners, and other possible stakeholders. This is a crucial step because this is where you need to convince the stakeholders, the merit of your new business model. From what channels you will be using for your car dealership (website, e-mail, social media), to how you will be running the daily business processes online, everything needs to be clear, and flawless. You must satisfy your stakeholders, so they give you the go-ahead you need to make the online shift.

Once your business stakeholders are in agreement with you, it is time to set the plan in motion. This is the practical step, and it needs to be performed with careful attention to every little detail. Although this is not an implementation stage, it is equally important, as this will determine how your dealership will practically operate online once it is up and running. This is the step where you will prepare for the concept of your new business model for your car dealership.

Designing the Concept

The concept of online operations for your car dealership should include everything a physical business includes. For starters, you need all the departments in your dealership on board, which will aid you in running online operations smoothly. For example, the Marketing Department will be the one to market your new business model, and it's features to your customers. Therefore, they must be aware of online marketing strategies, as well. In another example, the Finance Department will be the one that provides you with the cash inflow needed to devise strategies, implement, and efficiently run the online operations. They must be aware of all the costs associated with the online shift.

The next step in designing the concept of your online business is arranging the human resource needed for the shift. Make sure you have the needed team on hand for both technical and non-technical jobs needed for the shift.

The last step of the designing concept includes the evaluation of the timeline of Profit Returns for the online operations of your car dealership. Draw up a detailed timeline of when you expect your online operations to start generating sales. By having a clear understanding of this, you will be able to monitor your daily activities in the context of making a profit more accurately.

Setting up the Website

Setting up your website is one of the most important and critical processes you will have to carry out in your shift to online operation. For your dealership, you need a fully functional, and user-friendly website, to convert the hits/clicks on your website to actual sales.

Website Features

A company's website is the first impression when a customer visits. It retains the customer within seconds, and it has to be effective to capture leads. Therefore, some of the key features that your website should include are:

• Accessible from all devices (computers, mobile phones, and tablets)

• Contains virtual tours of the cars.

• Has an option, visible on top of the page to book an appointment with a salesperson, if needed.

• Has features, such as ChatBots.

The website of your car dealership needs to be presented in the form of a virtual shop that has all the cars available for virtual viewing with all the information about it.

Virtual Tour of the Cars

One of the most interesting and exciting features that you can add to your website is a virtual tour of the cars you're selling. In other words, your website needs a complete 3D look inside the car that the customer wishes to buy.

Another website of a dealership in Canada called Car360 is a great example of how helpful and effective a virtual car tour could be. On the website, all the major car brands are listed in clickable links. As you click, it directs you to a full 360-degree tour to the inside of the car, where you can easily zoom into areas to explore them like you are physically there. The website also has a search feature, which makes it easier to look for your desired car, and take the virtual tour.

Book an Appointment

'Booking an Appointment' is one of the most important features that your website could have. Although most of us are getting used to interaction less shopping experience, there are times when we need to talk to a real person. In regards to a car dealership, a customer would want to talk to a real person after the purchase decision is made, and it is time to discuss financing, leasing, or other payment methods. However, here is how things get different for an online car dealership. When it comes to having an online business, in the most real sense, all appointments made are not physical, but virtual. This means that once the appointment is made, the customer will be entertained via video call by a real person.

One way to do it is that once the customer clicks on the "Book an Appointment" option, he can be directed to put in his available date and time. Once done, the website can be configured to send an automatic link to Google Meet or a Zoom call. This way, the customer can have the option of having an interaction with a real person, without compromising on having a full online buying experience.

One of the most common things that a customer needs assistance for is financing. When the deal is done, and it's time to explore payment options, a customer always prefers a real person over a website virtually guiding him. To make this easier for the customer, a virtual appointment can be used to ease his worries. For example: If a customer decides to go for a lease, what you can do is show all the paperwork to the customer through a video call, send him copies of those documents so both of you can review it simultaneously, and go through all the points one by one via video call. Any questions that the customer may have, you can address them in real-time. That way, he will feel at ease when finally signing the documents, as he was able to interact with a real person throughout the process.

CRM (Customer Relationship Management) Features

The opposers of online businesses often argue that CRM is one thing that is impossible to obtain through online channels. Many believe that the only way to maintain a good relationship with your customers after the sale is made is through having personal contact with them.

However, with the advancement in technology, CRM is made possible and effective through online channels as well. Artificial Intelligence is one way to carry out CRM operations without compromising the personal touch of the old conventional method. An important feature that you can include on the website of your dealership is a Chat Box. This is an automatic chat service, where the customer is dealt with by pre-programmed responses from a bot, which answers like a real person. This is done through intelligently figuring out the most asked questions, and pre-setting their answers to look more real. For example, people visiting a website of a car dealership will most likely want to know their financing options or insurance plans. By knowing this, you can have your IT team prepare pre-set answers. These answers will be sent automatically to the customer via the chat option.

The process behind this is simple. Each answer is programmed to be sent at a certain keyword. To explain this, we will use the same example as above: in that case, a keyword could be 'insurance plan'. Now, any time a customer will type in this keyword into the chat box, the pre-programmed answer on this keyword would be sent to him. This will make the customer feel that their queries are being heard and answered.

By adding these features on your website, you are making sure that your dealership becomes an online business that doesn't require physical existence. Each feature will provide a unique action that was previously performed at the shop. By including all of these features together, you are also making sure that your dealership stands out among your competitors, and thus become the first choice for customers.

Covid-19 and Post Trauma Effects

One of the reasons why you need to think about making the shift to an online dealership is the prevailing situation of Covid-19. The Pandemic has taken the world by a storm. The world that we knew before no longer exists. As offices have taken a shift to "Work from Home", purchases of all kinds are taking a turn to just being online. While there are other reasons to turn your physical car dealership into an online experience, in the present times, the Corona pandemic is a major one.

One thing to note here is that this shift from physical to virtual all around will not magically come back to normalcy with the end of the virus. There is going to be a rippling effect that will last a lifetime. The post-traumatic effect will be the hardest one to come out of. People who have resorted to online channels for their purchases due to Covid-19 will most probably wouldn't want to go back to the old ways. This is because online channels are more convenient and prove to be cheaper for both the customer and the seller. This is why making the shift at the right time will help your dealership to rise above those who stayed in the roots, and refused to grow. It is the principle of evolution. Those who evolve with time remain, while those who don't go extinct.

In the end, when you do decide to make the shift to an online dealership, make sure that you are providing your customers with an exceptional online experience. The partiality often inconveniences the customer. Don't confuse them with having an online presence, but asking them to visit the store for so and so. Have an online presence that is able to deal with anything that the customer may need. Only then will you be able to stand out as the best car dealership among your close competitors.

Chapter 7
Conclusion

The world around is changing on a daily basis. The things that we could never have expected to happen have happened such as the Corona Virus Pandemic, which has taken the world by a storm. The pandemic also proved to be drastically alternating to many businesses, especially those that operated in the service industry and couldn't shift to an online platform.

The constant change of market trends, the continuous advancement in technology, and the new normal of online shopping could often seem overwhelming for businesses to keep track of and stay updated. The drastic shift to e-commerce of almost all the industries might look challenging for those businesses that are still operating physically, without an online presence.

However, it's extremely essential to alter your ways with the changing market trends, if you wish to survive in your industry. If nature teaches us anything, it's this: those that fail to evolve over time go extinct. Upgrading your day-to-day business operations with the changing trends is an integral part of your growth. In this book, we discussed how we can accurately and effectively shift your car dealership to an online platform. We learned about various ways to advertise and market our dealership and how we can use the online space to generate leads and increase our sales. It is understandable that with the abundance of information that I shared with you, the comprehension might have been hard. Therefore, in this chapter, I will conclusively give my readers a rundown of everything we discussed previously and we will end on a note of what we can expect from our future.

Strategy and Planning

It all starts with a business plan. The crux of your success lies in your strategic planning and the ways you aim to implement your core strategy. Before you start with your car dealership, it's essential that you collect some necessary statistics about the industry you're to operate in. Information is key and you can never be too prepared for business. In order to collect the required data for your car dealership, you can research on the following:

- Market analysis
- Market shares
- New entrants
- New models
- Customer retention
- Customer satisfaction index
- Market research
- Previous business plans
- Business investments
- Main objectives (e.g., to build a body shop or to expand shop)
- Human resources needed to deliver next year's goal
- Sales per month
- Budget reviews
- New year budgets (fixed and variable expenses)
- Customer acquisition cost
- Cost per lead
- Number of leads
- Conversion rate

Determining and setting your budget is another essential step that you need to carry out prior to starting your dealership. You can do so by dividing your dealership into preset departments and then allocating a certain budget to each one, as per their expected expenditure. A marketing budget should be a percentage of your revenue – anywhere from 5% to 10% according to NADA (National Automobile Dealers Association).

However, before you fill out the Marketing Budget Template, you should analyze what worked and what did not in terms of marketing. Explore all platforms such as Google Ads, Bing Ads, Instagram Ads, Facebook Ads, radio, newspaper, TV, private sales, direct mail, events, sponsorships, partnerships, and all the other options. In that sense, use previous years' data to analyze it (e.g., the cost per vehicle, number of leads per channel, and syndicated data such as CarGurus, Auto Trader, Kijiji, and others).

Traditional Means of Marketing are Going Extinct - Think Anew

My book has placed a high value on learning about marketing and the right channels to opt for because improving the sales of your dealership is the first step toward taking your car dealership to new heights. The only way to bring your dealership to the 21st century is to understand that slowly but surely, traditional marketing is dying. E-commerce and online operations have become the new normal and you have to make alterations if you wish to stay ahead in your industry.

While older mediums of advertisements, such as newspaper, radio, and TV have been the main source to get ads for decades, there has been a major shift to various online platforms. Although big companies still use TV commercials for their campaigns, many smaller businesses have written their success stories through advertising solely on online channels. Looking at the current trend, even the big companies have started marketing their products/services online and garnered a considerable amount of sales through that.

While TV is still quite a prevalent medium of advertisement, radio is almost meeting its end. I predict that the next disruption will happen when all vehicles start coming with the internet on them as that may dramatically alter radio's market share, as big national groups could start broadcasting all over the country like a national station. Listeners would be able to browse and tune to any radio station in the world. YouTube, Instagram IGTV (Instagram TV), and music apps, like Spotify, will play a big role in this scenario as most vehicles will have monitors coming as a standard feature. The newspaper is another medium that the current generation has forgone. Presently, people obtain news through social media, which is more accessible and easy to decipher. Even those who liked reading the newspaper are slowly shifting to reading news online through virtual newspapers. This opens up an avenue for businesses to adversities on those sites as well. This is an additional advantage to using non-traditional means of marketing.

So, it is established that traditional ways of marketing no longer work as effectively as they used to. Therefore, for your dealership to survive the test of changing times, you need to be watchful of the constantly altering trends and start to market your business on online channels such as social media (Facebook, Instagram, YouTube), Google Web, through emails and virtual newsletters.

Local Community Engagement

Along with the importance that I have relayed on

moving your car dealership's operations online and the impact of social media marketing on the success of your business, it's highly essential to understand that your success rests upon the local community's support. Community engagement plays a vital role in taking your dealership to new heights. At times, a good word of recommendation from a close friend works better than many vibrant and engaging pieces of advertisements. Having a close-knit community that supports your business could be highly impactful in generating more sales.

You have to construct the right image for your business. When it comes to building a long-term reputation in the local community, brand sponsorship and partnership should be part of your marketing strategy and plan. This additionally means to build, maintain, and enhance your relationships with other organizations within the community. Engagement with other businesses that are relevant to your dealership could go a long way for you.

To maximize the results and brand exposure, you have to engage and work actively with the organization to leverage your exposure to the community. Additionally, you should also allocate a specific budget for this task.

Moreover, you should engage all your employees to join you as a part of a dealership project. Remember, a united front is essential because it is likely that your staff members are also from the community. If they feel like they are a part of your brand, you will begin seeing positive effects rippling across the target market. That is why you must have everyone participating and engaging in utilizing the potential.

Social Media Is the Key to Modern Success

The role that social media plays in generating leads and increasing sales for many big and small businesses is unprecedented. In the past decade or so, there has been a gradual shift in the marketing paradigms. What was once just a service to communicate with friends and family has now become the most prominent advertising tool.

It is high time that car dealerships start to plan their shift toward this mega platform in order to evolve effectively with the changing business dynamics. You might wonder how a service-oriented intermediary, such as a car dealership uses platforms like Facebook or Instagram to market their services and products. There are certain technical or operational queries that might arise in your mind, like how will the delivery be possible? How can the inventory be shown? Social media for a car dealership is to create buzz, generate online traffic, and get the word going around about your dealership. You can also set up a *shop* on social media for people to take advantage of the option, especially for those who already know what they want to buy and don't need a physical visit. However, the use of social media just to market your service is also a great way to attract more customers into your shop.

In regard to social media marketing, the most important thing to consider is the outlet you will be using to market your dealership or set up your shop. As of today, your most adequate and effective options are:

- Facebook
- Instagram
- LinkedIn
- Snapchat
- Twitter

This book has already discussed in detail how you can create business pages for your dealership on the above-mentioned platforms and gain the help of these popular sites to generate more sales. Ultimately, social media marketing is one of the most impactful marketing tactics of present times. It's the most profit-generating branch of digital marketing and paves the way for a lot of advertisement opportunities in terms of using the digital medium to commercialize your product or service.

Getting Leads - Digitalizing Your Car Dealership's Advertisement

Digital marketing, as opposed to its older counterpart, television, has emerged far and wide in the business space over the last decade. One of the greatest benefits of digital marketing, in comparison to conventional marketing, is that you can easily carry out all the steps yourself, in a cost-efficient way.

TV ads may have been one of the most impactful means of advertisement for decades, but they are expensive. This is why they are slowly losing their place as the main medium of advertisement. The high cost makes it impossible for small businesses to advertise on TV. In contrast, digital marketing provides a relatively easy and cost-friendly route to market your products. Digitalizing your dealership's marketing strategies means relying solely on a digital platform to advertise your services and the cars in your inventory. Some ways to use the digital platform is to advertise through posting ad videos on various online channels (Facebook, YouTube, and Google). The best part about digital marketing is that you have the liberty to record, edit, and upload the ad video yourself, which cuts down costs by a huge margin. You can also use Google ads or social media sponsored ads to advertise about your dealership. The ad could be in a video or a simple image form.

Digital marketing is gaining popularity rapidly and deservingly so. With a grand shift of businesses to online platforms, a service-oriented industry such as a car dealership needs to follow suit. It is the general principle of evolution and a vital part of the product life cycle. To prevent declining after reaching maturity, you need to evolve and innovate with time. It is the right time to use digital marketing to get more leads for your car dealership and convert as many of your ad clicks to sales as possible.

Make the Final Shift Online

Once you have learned the importance and how-tos of operating your dealership via an online platform, it's time to make the final shift. Why is it essential for a car dealership to move the majority portion of its business online? Because most of the buyers in the present times are millennials and prefer to shop online from the comfort of their homes. With this kind of buying environment, companies have realized the importance of providing the customers with online channels, not only to explore options but also to purchase and avail the after-sales services.

In respect of a car dealership, making a complete shift to online operations could be tricky. However, with correct planning and effective implementation, it is possible. The idea here is to devise a step-by-step plan properly, follow through carefully, and implement each step with effectiveness and efficiency. Briefly, the steps involved in making the shift online are:

- Designing the concept
- Setting up the website - adequately devise, pick, and implement the features that you'd like your

website to have, such as virtual tours of the cars and booking an appointment)

- Establishing workable CRM (Customer Relationship Management)

Another thing to consider here is the global pandemic that we're all facing currently. Amid the COVID-19 fiasco, almost all businesses have taken a turn to online platforms. One thing to note here is that this shift from physical to virtual will not magically come back to normalcy with the end of the virus. There is going to be a rippling effect that will last a lifetime. Therefore, the pandemic is an additional reason why this is the right time for you to switch to an online presence for your car dealership.

This final online shift also has to be an exceptional online experience. Beware of partiality as it inconveniences and confuses the customer. Your car dealership's online platform (website, pages, and more) needs to be equipped with everything a customer may need from start to end of their buying process. Only by doing so, you'll be able to stand out amongst your competitors.

What the Future Holds for Your Dealership

In the next years, we will experience and see a revolution in the automotive industry. Transitioning from the fossil engine vehicles to electric self-autonomous driving vehicles. In less than a decade, electric vehicles will be more affordable than fossil vehicles. Not to mention, some countries and cities will create restrictions for fossil vehicles to circulate and tax incentives for eco-friendly electric vehicles will impact on purchase decisions. Conversion packages and service to turn the fossil vehicle into electricity will also be offered.

The ownership of a vehicle will change. Timeshare and apps like Uber and others will grow exponentially over the course of the next few years. Leasing will increase and new modalities will come up. The online purchase will definitely take over the traditional in-store purchases, with the added feature of home delivery.

Online auctions for used vehicles, nowadays only available and opened to dealerships and not to the general public, will be opened to everyone. This, in turn, will have a severe impact on dealership margins when buying and selling a used vehicle. Companies like TradeRev, for instance, will see a great impact from this. New dot com companies, like Clutch and Curbie, will grow and grab a significant market share on used vehicles.

Although these are my informed guesses, I could surely say that the future of online car dealerships looks quite promising. This is why I hope you have enjoyed this book; and the content and insights that I provided could help your dealership to get more leads and sales.

Here is my contact information for any further assistance or question.

Richard Halbe

richard.halbe@gmail.com
www.halbe.ca

RICHARD HALBE

www.ingramcontent.com/pod-product-compliance
Lightning Source LLC
Chambersburg PA
CBHW022045190326
41520CB00008B/712